What About Now?

Reminders for Being
in the Moment

Gina Lake

Endless Satsang Foundation

www.radicalhappiness.com

ISBN: 9781442151598

INTRODUCTION

This book was created from short excerpts from seven previous books about awakening out of the egoic mind and living in the moment. It is intended to help you do just that. The excerpts are reminders that can be read in any order. We all need reminders to be more present in our lives to our real experience and ignore what is negative and detracts from true happiness, which is the chatter of the egoic mind.

The aspect of mind that I'm calling the *egoic mind* is what we think of as our own thoughts. They are primarily thoughts about ourselves and others: beliefs, opinions, and other conditioned ideas as well as desires, memories, fantasies, hopes, fears, and dreams. They seem to belong to us, but they actually belong to the false self, or ego, and don't contribute to our lives, although they make for the drama that this character that we know ourselves as experiences.

You are reading this book because you are ready to wake up from the drama of being *you* and start living as the real you—Essence—which has been here all along, pretending to be this character. The trouble with being this character is that it suffers because it has a lot of false beliefs and negative ideas and misunderstandings about life. The good news is that you don't have to believe the thoughts that this character was given, in the form of conditioning. You can, instead, live as Essence, spontaneously and in response to the moment rather than in response to the egoic mind, and life will go very well!

That may be hard for the ego to trust, but it is the truth, which we are all meant to discover. This book is meant to help you discover and trust who you really are so that you can live as that instead of unconsciously responding to your conditioning and the ego's drives for more of everything. The ego's appetite for more is never satisfied, so we suffer. When we learn to live in the moment, we discover that life provides us with what we need and that we have never needed what the ego promises in order to be happy. We discover that, indeed, happiness has always been here in this simple moment.

ENJOY THE SIMPLE PLEASURES

When we are just present to what we are experiencing, we notice all sorts of sensory details that are usually overlooked. The surprising thing is the amount of joy that can be felt in experiencing the simplest of things fully: the warmth of the sun, the softness of fabric against the body, the brilliancy of the blue sky, the squishiness of the earth below our feet, the scent of a pine tree, the buzz of something in the distance. The ego isn't satisfied with these experiences because it isn't satisfied with anything. We aren't satisfied with such things either when we are identified with the ego because identification with the mind keeps us from fully experiencing them. But what *is* life but the experience of these simple things?

WHAT IS THE IMPACT OF SENSORY EXPERIENCE?

The joy of being in the Now goes beyond the pleasure of the senses. To go deeper into Essence, there is another very important step, once we are fully sensing without the interference of the mind's commentary, and that is to fully experience the *effect* that sensory experience has on our Being. When you look at that beautiful flower or hear that bird's song, what impact does it have on your internal energetic experience? What is your Being experiencing? Or another way of asking this is, What is Essence's experience of this moment?

SURRENDER THE NEED TO KNOW

What makes the choice of being in the moment difficult is that we have to surrender our need to know. The ego gives us a false sense of knowing, which is comforting, even though the ego doesn't really know where life is going or what will happen next. So all we really have to surrender is the *pretense* of knowing, not actual knowing. The truth is we don't know what the next moment holds. That's both the challenge of being in the Now and, actually, the true joy of it. To be in the moment, we have to be willing to just be and to respond naturally to what arises out of the flow, without pretending to know what to do next or what will happen. The thing is, you have never known what was going to happen or what to do next. Admitting that you don't know allows you to move out of your egoic mind and into the moment, where true happiness, peace, and alignment with Essence and its intentions are possible.

IGNORE THE VOICE IN YOUR HEAD

The good news is that nearly all of our thoughts are unnecessary, not just a few of them. That makes discriminating between them much easier. We don't have to go sorting through our thoughts for the right ones. We just need to recognize that egoic thought belongs to the false self and is therefore false and unworthy of our attention. We can disregard all the thoughts that relate to *me* and *my story* and all the other chatter, judgments, opinions, memories, fantasies, dreams, desires, likes, dislikes, doubts, fears, complaints, and other negativity of the ego. What we are left with is a functional mind that still knows how to read, calculate, use a computer, drive a car, follow a map or instructions, and do all the other things the mind was designed for. What a relief it is to realize that the voice in our head can be ignored! Can you trust this? Just start noticing how you don't need any of your thoughts to experience the present moment and do what you need to do. See for yourself.

FEEL YOUR BEING REJOICING IN LIFE

When you really take in the beauty and anything else you are experiencing through your senses, you feel how your Being is rejoicing and celebrating this moment, and you experience this energetically. This subtle energetic experience is the experience of the Heart, or Essence, of your true Self. This subtle joy, expansion, relaxation, yes to life is the radical happiness that comes from experiencing life as Essence experiences it. That subtle experiencing is ongoing and ever-present, but it often isn't noticed because thinking is more obvious and compelling, even though thinking is actually less rewarding.

NOTICE HOW LIFE COMES OUT OF THE NOW

The more accustomed we become to being present, the more we begin to live as Essence, which is a free and joyful experience. The Now is not just a place of sensory experience, although that is sufficiently rich, but where life comes out of. If we aren't paying attention to the Now, we might miss what life is trying to bring about through us. We can follow the egoic mind's plans and ideas for our life if we want to, but something else right here and now has a plan, and that plan will be much more satisfying than anything the ego has to offer.

DROP OUT OF YOUR MIND AND INTO THE NOW

Surrendering to life isn't hard at all. It happens simply and naturally whenever we stop paying attention to our mind's version of life and start paying attention to life, itself, as it is coming out of the Now. There's something else to do besides think! And that is to notice, to be aware of what is happening now. Notice, look, feel, listen, sense, and give yourself fully to the experience you are having, and you will drop into the Now.

THOUGHTS ARE NOT IMPORTANT

For the most part, thoughts are stabs at truth and tell us little about how to live in the present moment. Instead, they keep us at arm's length from the moment. They keep us living in a mentally fabricated reality, the realm of ideas, instead of the Now. They interfere with life rather than enhance it. This is contrary to our deeply held belief that thoughts are important, relevant, and meaningful. Somehow, we have been convinced of this rather than the opposite—that they keep us from reality and Truth. But that is what we are here to discover! Thoughts are the structure of the ego and what hold it in place. Without them, the ego wouldn't exist. This belief— that thoughts are important, valuable, and meaningful—is the lynchpin that, when removed, causes the whole game to fall apart. And where we land is smack dab in reality, in this alive moment.

HOW IS ESSENCE MOVING YOU NOW?

How is Essence moving you now, in this moment? That will give you a clue to what its intentions are. You discover Essence's intentions, not by looking in your mind, but by noticing what is going on in the present moment. Thoughts of "I want" might also be arising in the moment, but what else is here? What is here that is more true and real than any thought?

EXPERIENCE YOUR TRUE SELF IN THE MOMENT

Who you really are can only be experienced in the present moment, not through thought. When we move our attention away from thought onto anything else, we land in the present moment, and the experience of being present is the experience of our true self. This experience is one of love, compassion, acceptance, joy, and contentment. When you feel these, you know you are identified with your true self rather than the ego. When you feel the opposite, discontentment and unhappiness, you know you are identified with the ego, with your thoughts.

EXPERIENCE WHAT YOU ARE EXPERIENCING

Experiencing what you are experiencing and experiencing your thoughts are very different realities, very different experiences. When you are experiencing what you are experiencing, you are at peace, relaxed, content, absorbed, with no thoughts about *me* or how *I* am doing, or any other stories, which are the ego's version of reality. Instead of experiencing reality, the ego tells a story about it, and that becomes its reality.

DON'T LISTEN TO THE EGOIC MIND'S PROMISES

The egoic mind tries to get you to hurry through life so that you don't experience life because if you actually experience life, the ego, your sense of self, disappears! So the ego hurries you on to the next moment and promises a future where you will finally be happy and able to rest. But that future never comes! It's a shell game: The mind promises you a better life if you listen to it, while it takes you out of the only thing that is real: the present moment. That's not a good trade-off. The present moment is vibrant, alive, rich, and ever-changing, regardless of whatever the actual content is. This vibrancy, aliveness, and richness are the only things that will ever fulfill you. What is unreal—thoughts, fantasies, and promises of the future—can never fulfill you, but only take you away from what can.

JUMP INTO THE EXPERIENCE WITH BOTH FEET

Love comes from jumping into experience fully and being willing to really have the experience you are having. Every moment is an opportunity to jump in with both feet, without holding back by evaluating the experience. The egoic mind inserts itself in every moment, or tries to, by evaluating it, worrying about it, or telling a story about it. This commentary doesn't enhance life or keep us safe, but simply distracts us from the experience and prevents us from being fully involved with it. Most people have one foot in their minds, so to speak, and one foot in their experience. This doesn't feel the same at all as having both feet in the experience.

CHOOSE WHERE YOUR ATTENTION
GOES AND WHAT YOU BELIEVE

We have the freedom to choose what we give our
attention to and what we believe about ourselves, our
situation, others, and life. This is a tremendous
responsibility, as it determines to a great extent what
our experience of life will be. No matter what your
circumstances are, you have the freedom to accept
them, which simply means to not argue with reality,
but allow yourself to have the experience you are
having—because you are having it!

BE HERE IN THIS SIMPLE MOMENT

When the moment is stripped of the past, the future, opinions, beliefs, and desires, life becomes very simple. The ego doesn't like that, of course, because it likes complexity, problems, and drama, all of which it creates. You can have the complicated life the ego creates, or you can have an uncomplicated one. But just know that you don't have to have complications, drama, problems, or dissatisfaction. You can just be here, now, in the moment, uncluttered by thoughts about *me,* what *I* believe, *my* past and future, and what *I* want. You really don't need any of them.

GIVE YOUR LOVE AWAY

We have everything we need because all we need is love, and everyone has an unlimited supply of that. Not everyone feels love, but it's always there and available to give to others. The way we experience this unlimited supply of love is by giving it away. That's counter intuitive, which is why it may seem like there isn't enough. When you believe you need to get love from outside yourself, that sense of lack stops the flow from happening from inside you. The belief in needing love becomes a self-fulfilling prophesy: You believe you need it because you aren't experiencing it, and in trying to get it, you fail to give it. We can't really do two things at once. If we are relating to someone, we are either giving our full attention (love) to them or trying to get something from them. We are either in Essence (giving attention) or in ego (trying to get attention). These are very different states of consciousness, and they result in a very different experience.

LOVE WHAT IS OR SUFFER

Loving and embracing whatever is going on is the only sane choice. The alternative is to reject it and suffer over it. If rejecting it could change what is, then that might make sense, but rejection only causes us to be unhappy. Throughout most of our evolution, we don't realize we have a choice between suffering and not suffering. We are programmed to listen to the mind, which rejects something about every moment. It is designed to do that. We don't realize that its voice isn't a voice of truth and wisdom. We really believe that what it believes about the moment is what *I* believe. What a blessing when we reach a point in our evolution when we see that we don't have to agree with the mind's perceptions, when we see that these perceptions have only caused us to suffer and feel negative and small, narrow and contracted.

CHOOSE HOW YOU RESPOND TO LIFE

Freedom is truly a state of mind or, rather, a state of no mind, or ignoring the mind's complaints about life. You are already free and always have been. You have been given this great gift of choice: the freedom to choose how you see life and respond to it. As a result, everyone eventually learns to see life through the eyes of the true self and ignore the false self's version, which is the source of all suffering. Happiness is under your control more than you may realize. You have more power than you may think— you have the power to *not* think, to ignore your thoughts, and to experience the gift that this life is.

NOTICE THE JOY OF BEING IN THE NOW

Because thinking is our default position as humans, we have to learn to notice what else is present besides thought. We have to learn to notice what is real and true in the present moment. We have to train ourselves to pay attention to the subtle joy, expansion, relaxation and yes of Essence as it enjoys life through us. This subtle experience becomes less subtle and easier to notice the more we put our attention on it rather than on thought. Then, the mind becomes quieter, softer, and more in the background.

LOVE YOUR EXPERIENCE

You can tell a sad story about life if you like, but it won't be the truth. Life will allow you to feel sad for as long as you wish. But eventually you'll discover that there's another possibility, and that is to embrace life as it is, with all its messiness and difficulties and to love it for the experience that it provides you for now, because that's what is happening. You love life just because that's what is happening. And you love your experience just because that's what is happening and because the alternative—to hate it, be angry, be sad, or reject it—is just not acceptable.

DON'T GO WHERE THE MIND WANTS YOU TO GO

When you realize the egoic mind's game, you are at a choice point. Where do you put your attention? If you want to wake up out of the suffering created by the egoic mind, you have to choose to not go where it wants you to go. You have to choose this again and again, in every moment, until it becomes a choiceless choice, one that is automatically made out of love for Essence. With repeated experiences of Essence, choosing Essence becomes increasingly easy.

FIND THE OPPORTUNITY IN THE EXPERIENCE

There is a wisdom and purposefulness behind what you experience, even difficult experiences. When you say yes to an experience, you are able to align with that purposefulness and find fulfillment in that experience. Every experience is an opportunity to grow, learn, evolve, and become wiser and more loving. That's how Essence views difficult experiences. Acceptance allows you to tap into the potential for good that an experience holds. It allows you to benefit from the experience and move through it as gracefully as possible. And it allows you to feel the joy Essence feels in having that experience and every other one. It aligns you with Essence's plan for you and the role that experience is playing in your plan so that you can grow from it, as Essence intends.

NOTICE EXPANSION AND CONTRACTION

What are you thinking right now and how does it affect you? Does it expand or contract your consciousness? Some thoughts cause us to become more contracted and ego-identified, while others cause us to become more expanded and identified with Essence. Those that do the latter could be said to be truer than the former. This is because truth puts us in touch with Truth, or what's real, while what is not true puts us in touch with what is not real: the ego.

TRUST THE HEART, NOT YOUR DOUBTS AND FEARS

What's so hard about trusting the Heart, when the Heart actually has a very good reputation? You don't hear people saying, "Be careful—don't trust your Heart too much!" Rather, they tell you to trust your Heart. What keeps you from trusting your Heart then? The answer is: thoughts of doubt and worry that stir up negative emotions, especially fear. Fear and other negative emotions make your thoughts seem true. The ego tricks you into believing its thoughts instead of your Heart by producing negative feelings, tension, and contraction in your body, which make your thoughts seem true and necessary to your survival. Pretty tricky, isn't it?

NOTICE THE DETAILS OF YOUR SENSORY EXPERIENCE

The joy in being present is in noticing the light reflecting off the silverware, the specks of dust floating in the sunlight, the contentment on your dog's face, the way the folds of the curtain fall, the shadows cast by the rocks, the clouds changing shapes, the smell of fallen leaves, the taste of butter on bread. There is infinite variety available in this moment to enjoy, if you notice, but you have to be willing to notice the small things, the details, because they are often what sets the present moment apart from other moments.

THE RICHNESS OF LIFE COMES
THROUGH THE SENSES

The ego sees something it has seen hundreds of times, and it assumes it knows that thing. The egoic mind might think about that thing, analyze or judge it, or just overlook it. The ego skips over an experience and substitutes thoughts for experience. In assuming it has already had that experience, the ego misses experiencing the moment altogether, which is where the juiciness and aliveness of life is. The ego's mental world is a dry one. Its world lacks connection with real sensory experience. The richness in being alive comes through our senses. When we experience what is coming into our senses, we feel alive, and we feel the joy Essence feels in being alive.

GIVE UP YOUR THOUGHTS OF WANTING

Giving up our desires is nothing more than giving up a thought of wanting. Giving up our thoughts of wanting simply means not giving those thoughts our attention—ignoring them. Such thoughts have never helped us to be happier or even helped us to get what we thought we wanted. Wanting isn't valuable, so giving up wanting is giving up nothing except for our suffering. Are you willing to give up your suffering? That's a question worth examining because, the truth is, the ego doesn't want you to give up your suffering, since the ego has no purpose without suffering.

NOTICE THAT ACCEPTANCE IS ALREADY HERE

Acceptance is a quality of our true nature. The Awareness that we are, Essence, is naturally accepting. It accepts because it loves life—all of life and every possible experience it might have through us. It is so in love with life and with the possibilities that life brings that it embraces even the difficult experiences. It is curious and anxious to experience everything that life (its creation) offers it. It jumps into creation with eagerness and joy. We are able to feel this joy if we are willing to. Often we are too caught up in the ego's rejection of life to notice the acceptance and love of life that is the ongoing experience of who we really are.

NOTHING IS MISSING FROM THIS MOMENT

The only thing that can keep us from being happy is a thought. What a revolutionary truth that is! The kind of thought that interferes with happiness the most is a thought of lack, which is at the base of all desire. If we didn't think something was missing or lacking about ourselves, someone else, our situation, or life, we wouldn't be unhappy. Unhappiness is caused by believing that something is missing that we need to be happy. This *belief* is what makes us unhappy, not the fact that something is or isn't here right now.

PUT YOUR ATTENTION ON WHAT
LOVES LIFE

We can experience love for the gift of being alive and for being able to experience the present moment. This is the love Essence feels as it lives life through us. What a wonder the physical body is! This sense of wonder and gratitude for life, the body, and other living things is love. The Being that we are is in awe of life. When we move our attention onto that which loves life, we feel complete. Nothing more is needed in the moment than that. What a surprise that life can be this simple and this complete!

ALLOW OTHERS TO BE AS THEY ARE

Relating from Essence is very different from relating from the ego. When you relate from Essence, the dominant feeling is acceptance. You allow others to be the way they are. In fact, you celebrate how they are. This doesn't mean you might not dislike something about them, but the general feeling toward them is that everything is just right the way it is. This feeling of acceptance and allowing toward another is love in its simplest, most unadulterated (by conditioning) form. Love in its most basic form is allowing. You allow the person to be exactly the way he or she is without any reservations or desires for anything to be different than it is.

NOTICE WHAT IS NOTICING

Notice what is aware of your hands and the aliveness in your hands. What is looking out of your eyes and noticing? What is noticing is not what thinks. Noticing is separate from thinking. Noticing is silent, allowing, non-evaluative, and simply experiencing what it is noticing. You may also experience some rejoicing in this noticing, since being aware of life is essentially a joyous experience. What a miracle it is to be alive and aware and to have a vehicle for experiencing life! Without this body and without the consciousness connected to this body, we couldn't have even the simplest experience.

NOTICE THE MIND TRYING TO CO-OPT EXPERIENCE

Watch the mind as it tries, in every moment, to co-opt experience by translating it into a story. It tries to draw you away from experience into a mental world that simulates experience. It tries to draw you into an imagined story about the experience. If it succeeds, that story becomes your experience. If you agree to go to this mental world, feelings will also arise and add reality to this world, but it is still a mental world.

KNOW THAT IT IS ALL GOOD

What if you saw every person who comes into your life and every experience you have as exactly what you need? Who knows why that person or experience is in your life? But you can trust that it is good, not always easy perhaps, but always good. What if you really knew that it was all good? We all eventually discover this. Why wait? Why not start believing this right now? The ego believes the opposite, but where has that gotten you? When we align with something other than the ego, we discover that life is indeed good. Everything can bring us closer to love and our true nature.

LOVE WHAT IS EVEN WHEN YOU PREFER SOMETHING ELSE

Loving what is, is not dependent on liking it. It's much easier to love whatever is happening when you realize that it's okay to prefer that something else be happening. Loving what is only requires that you jump into whatever is happening and experience it fully, whether you like it or not. Essence loves experience, and that is all you need to love to be happy.

GIVE YOUR ATTENTION TO SOMETHING BESIDES THOUGHTS

We are always paying attention to something. Most people pay most of their attention to what they are thinking and a minimal amount to what is going on around them. What they perceive about the world and what they experience is highly colored by what they are thinking. This is like seeing the world through a pair of glasses colored by conditioning: beliefs, ideas, desires, fears, dreams, preferences, memories, and opinions. These thoughts don't help us function more effectively in the world. At best, they don't interfere too much; at worst, they drain our energy and efficiency, slant our perceptions, and interfere with tapping into the wisdom within us that is available in every moment.

TRUST LIFE TO BE THE WAY IT IS

You can trust life to be the way it really is. What you can't trust is for it to be different than the way it is. In other words, you can't trust it to be the way the ego wants it to be. We can really trust life to be unpredictable, always changing, and challenging. We can't trust it to be predictable, the same, and easy, which is what the ego would like. Because life isn't the way the ego would like it to be, it proclaims it untrustworthy, but life is just the way it is—and you can trust that.

STAY IN THE EXPERIENCE WITHOUT A STORY

When you are in the flow, you experience whatever you are experiencing without telling a story about it. Thoughts may arise, but you recognize them as thoughts, as an attempt on the part of the ego to define the moment because that is what it tries to do. Meanwhile, you just stay in the experience of the moment, which is forever shifting into something else. When you are in the flow, you know yourself as that which is aware of thoughts, not someone who is thinking them.

YOU DON'T NEED YOUR EGOIC MIND
TO FUNCTION

You think you need your thoughts and feelings to function. You think they are you. But you don't need them, and they aren't you. They are part of the conditioned, false self that you *think* of yourself as, but they aren't what is alive in you and living this life and experiencing this moment. What is experiencing this moment, including what is aware of contraction over identification with thought, is who you are. It is very silent, though, unlike the egoic mind, which chatters away constantly. The real you is the Silent Experiencer who is alive and having the experience you are having.

DON'T FIGHT THE FLOW

The moment, the Now, is like a river that carries you forward, ever-changing and ever moving. You either flow with the moment or reject it and fight it, but that doesn't stop the flow; it only determines your experience of it. When you glide along with the flow, the experience is joyous, as you are able to experience the Source's joy in the moment it has created. When you fight the flow, you experience tension, anger, and dis-ease.

BE IN THE NOW, NOT IN YOUR THOUGHTS ABOUT IT

Surrender, or acceptance, allows you to experience life as it is unfolding, instead of experiencing your resistance to it. When you are identified with the ego, you aren't experiencing life, but your resistance to it. You're actually missing the experience of the Now because you're not in the Now, but in your thoughts about it, and that is a very different experience.

FIND THE PLACE WHERE NOTHING IS LACKING

The ego desires love, while Essence is love. When you are aligned with Essence, there is no desiring— not for love or anything else. The experience of Essence is an experience of completion, not lack. Therefore, any desire for love comes from the ego, which has difficulty experiencing the love that is always present, underlying all life. The ego doesn't feel love (Essence does), so it doesn't feel loved. The emptiness or lack is within the ego, not outside of it.

QUIET THE MIND BY BEING PRESENT TO WHAT YOU ARE DOING

When you are present to what you are doing, you are rewarded by a quiet mind, or at least a mind that remains in the background. That's a great relief. You don't have to listen to the negativity, complaints, arguments, confusion, fear, worries, and old worn-out stories of the egoic mind. If they are there, they seem more like a bad radio station in the background instead of about you. They don't seem personal. Being present to what you are doing quiets the mind, and that is its own reward. Relief from the egoic mind and immersion in Essence can turn an activity that you *think* is unpleasant into a very pleasant one.

DON'T STRENGTHEN THE *I*

Seeing the strength of the *I* and not strengthening it by not identifying with it or giving it a voice is a very powerful spiritual practice. And it does take practice before dis-identification from the ego becomes more our usual state than identification. We have to see that story spun by the egoic mind again and again before we begin to see ourselves as that which is aware of the story instead of the storyteller.

LOVE WHAT IS BECAUSE IT'S THE ONLY EXPERIENCE YOU'VE GOT

If the experience you are having is the right experience—and it is—then you might as well love it. It makes no sense to do anything else. It's the only thing you've got! You don't have any other experience but this one right now. The ego pretends that another experience is possible, but it isn't. That's the core lie. The egoic mind affects the experience you are having, coloring it with its stories, images, fears, desires, and perceptions, but you are still only having *this* experience.

ENJOY YOUR EXPERIENCE OR DON'T CHOOSE IT

In the egoic state of consciousness, when you are engaged in an activity, you are usually thinking about something else. If that weren't the case, you would drop into the flow, and you might not decide to do that activity. If you allow yourself to really experience the activity you are engaged in, either you would find yourself enjoying it or, from the place of Essence, you would choose differently. Either is a much better outcome than not being present to what you are doing and not enjoying it.

THE EGO ISN'T THE ONLY PLAYER HERE

The ego doesn't perceive that anything worthwhile is coming out of the flow. It discounts or disregards many of the insights, solutions, and urges to act that arise from Essence. The ego assumes it's the only player, and it convinces us of this too. It may seem that way because the flow's timing is not what the ego would like. The flow has its own timing, which is not revealed ahead of time. The ego assumes it needs to take control of life because it often seems like nothing is happening, and it's very unhappy with nothing happening. Almost anything seems better than that. The ego is at odds with the natural ebb and flow of life, and it pushes and tries to make life conform to its schedule. It's impatient with life as it is. However, the flow has a plan, which unlike the ego's, will bring you the life you were meant for.

TAKE CONTROL OF YOUR EXPERIENCE
OF REALITY

Your attention is important. It determines your experience of reality. You have a choice about what you give your attention to, once you realize you have a choice. Life is transformed by this realization. It's really very simple: Choosing to listen to the egoic mind takes you out of the moment and misleads and misguides you, while ignoring the mind brings you into the moment, where life is happening and wisdom and guidance are available.

PLEASURE IS DEPENDENT ON HOW PRESENT YOU ARE

The more we go in the direction of Essence and away from the ego, the more pleasure we experience, because pleasure is largely dependent on how present we are to whatever we are doing. Anything can be pleasurable if we are present to it without the interference of the egoic mind. The simplest things are pleasurable when we are present to them, even things we generally don't like. Being present is one of the secrets to happiness. The more we drop out of our egoic mind and into our senses, the more pleasure our senses deliver. Pleasure actually points the way Home.

GET LOST IN EXPERIENCE

The secret to enjoying what you are doing is to get lost in it, to get involved in it. That means getting all your senses involved in it or, more accurately, noticing how all your senses *are* involved in it. Noticing sensory experience takes you out of your egoic mind (your functional mind is still available) and into the experience you are having. When you are present to the experience you are having, you are in the moment, and that is when you experience Presence, or Essence. The experience of Essence is highly pleasurable, so no matter what you are doing, if you are present to it, it will be enjoyable.

COME INTO THE NOW BY NOTICING
THE ALIVENESS

Your hands are alive, and that aliveness can be felt. Take a moment and just feel that aliveness. It's experienced subtly, like a vibration or tingling or warmth. Notice how that aliveness is not only in your hands, but also throughout your body. Can you feel it in your face? Your scalp? Your feet? Your arms? Your thighs? Your chest? Every part of your body is alive, and that aliveness can be felt subtly when you pay attention to it. Paying attention to the aliveness will automatically bring you into the Now. Experiencing life brings you into life and brings you *to* life, you could say.

MAKE ACCEPTANCE A HABIT

Being accepting, like being loving, is another simple thing you can do in any moment to evoke Essence and bring yourself into the flow. Acceptance is a quality of Essence, and when your attitude or behavior reflects acceptance, you drop into Essence and the flow. To stay in the flow, you have to continue to be accepting. You can learn to make acceptance your natural response to life. The more you practice acceptance, the easier it becomes, although effort is needed at first to overcome the ego's automatic resistance to life and to whatever is happening.

NOTICE THE IDEAS THE MIND SPINS
ABOUT THE NOW

To experience the Now, we merely have to notice what is happening in the present moment without our interpretations, opinions, judgments, beliefs, or concepts about what we are experiencing. This may sound difficult, but all it takes is a shift from giving our full attention to our thoughts to *noticing* our thoughts. In addition to noticing our thoughts, noticing whatever else is present without interpreting it, judging it, or telling a story about it brings us into the Now and can keep us there as long as we continue to notice without interpreting or telling stories about what we are noticing. However, once any judgment, opinion, or belief is considered and not just noticed, we are back in the mind and identified with the ego again, instead of with Essence.

ACCEPT THAT YOU DON'T LIKE WHAT IS HAPPENING (IF YOU DON'T)

Accepting what is happening in the moment isn't as difficult as you may think because accepting it doesn't mean you have to like it. All you have to do is accept that you don't like what's happening, if that is the case. Accepting this moment just means you are willing to let it be the way it is. After all, what other choice do you have, since it is the way it is?

GIVE YOUR ATTENTION TO THE QUALITIES OF ESSENCE

When we are aligned with Essence, our experience of the moment changes. Our boundaries soften, we may feel a sense of expansion, and the sense of *me* falls into the background or disappears altogether. Peace, contentment, acceptance, gratitude, compassion, love, and any number of other positive qualities may arise. These qualities are indications of Essence. When we give our attention to these qualities, the experience of them increases.

NOTICE WHAT IS HAPPENING NOW

Notice what is arising now… and now… and now. Life is very interesting, very alive, and very dynamic. Every moment is unique. Something is always happening, and often it happens *through* you. If you are being receptive, you will catch not only what wants to move through you, but also what is moving through others. If you are aligned with Essence, you will recognize Essence being expressed in others and benefit from that. What a joy to see Essence everywhere perfectly, although unpredictably, performing this dance of life.

LOOK FROM ESSENCE'S EYES

To discover the goodness of life, you merely have to look from eyes other than the ego's. The ego sees nearly everything as flawed or bad. Even what the ego likes, it likes only for a time before judgment sets in and the ego becomes disgruntled with it. You won't find beauty, goodness, or love by looking through the ego's eyes. When you do find these, you are looking through Essence's eyes, which see only beauty, goodness, and love: When the branch moves in the wind, it sees the wind loving the branch and the branch loving the wind. When the sun comes up or goes down, it sees love in that. When a hummingbird dips its beak into a flower or a raven flies overhead, it sees love in that. Love is all around, when you have eyes for it.

WHAT KEEPS YOU FROM ENJOYING WHATEVER YOU ARE DOING?

Whatever you are doing, enjoy it! You have another option, of course, which is to not enjoy it. Notice what keeps you from enjoying whatever you are doing. It's your thoughts, isn't it? Even if you are experiencing pain, for instance, or something unpleasant, like going to the dentist, if you don't listen to any negative thoughts, fears, complaints, and desires related to that, you won't suffer. You will just have the experience.

FIND SOMETHING LOVABLE ABOUT
THIS MOMENT

The alternative to rejecting something about the way things are, which is what the ego does, is finding something to love about the way things are. There is always something to love in every moment. Can you find a sensation, something of beauty, or a sound that is loveable? Is peace here, even just a sliver? Is love? Is contentment? Is the universe holding together? Being happy or not being happy is largely a matter of what we focus on. When you find yourself struggling against life, stop and notice what is beautiful and loveable. And don't just stop with one thing; find another and another. Life can be lived from a place of celebration and gratitude instead of from a place of rejection. It is your choice.

NOTICE HOW UNTRUSTWORTHY THE MIND IS

Despite the impotence of the egoic mind, we trust it. It's a familiar old "friend." But when we look closely, we discover that the egoic mind isn't much of a friend. It often scares us and belittles us until we feel compelled to listen to it. It convinces us we can't trust life, that we are silly to do so, and that it has the answers to life. We trust the egoic mind out of habit, without examining whether it is trustworthy or not. When we observe the mind, we discover just how untrustworthy it is. It causes us to make poor choices and to feel negatively about ourselves, others, and life. And we don't see that our own mind has done that. That's how strong the programming is around believing our egoic mind. When we begin to question our thoughts, however, the whole house of cards collapses. How is it we didn't see this sooner? Indeed. The programming is tricky. That's the thing about programming—we aren't supposed to see through it!

FOLLOW YOUR HEART

What we love and most deeply want to do shows up in the moment as an impulse, inspiration, or urge to do something. We may think about that inspiration or urge, or express it verbally, but what makes our Heart sing doesn't show up initially as a thought. What is most meaningful for us to do shows up as a feeling of wanting to do something, not as the thought "I want…." That's the difference. "Follow your Heart" means follow your feelings. However, those feelings aren't the emotions that come from the ego, but the deeper drives of Essence. We *feel* that something is right or true, and that feeling is an intuition, not an emotion. Following our emotions can get us into a lot of trouble, but following these intuitive feelings brings us happiness and fulfillment.

GIVE UP STRIVING TO BE HAPPY

When we are able to see the ego's striving for what it is—a frantic, egocentric attempt to be someone special, to be safe, to be admired, and so on—then we can begin to let go of striving. It is only the ego that needs the things the ego wants. The ego wants what it wants for itself, not for love or a higher purpose. Who we really are has no need of anything, but already has everything it needs to be happy. Striving is actually what makes us feel lacking, as if we don't have what we need to be happy. We strive because we believe we need something to be happy, when we have never needed anything at all, and nothing "out there" will ever satisfy us anyway. The ego takes us on a wild goose chase. It convinces us that we need to be someone and have our life look a certain way to be happy, and we don't. We don't suffer because we don't have what we want, but because we believe we need something other than what we already have to be happy.

LIFE IS ALWAYS GOOD

Life is always good, and we are always having the experience we need. If life doesn't seem that way, you are listening to the mind's sad or negative story about life. This kind of suffering is so unnecessary. When we drop out of our egoic mind and into this simple moment, we discover the truth about life. Life can be lived very well from this place of Presence, or being in the Now, because Presence is what is real, and the ego and its thoughts are not real. The good news is we have never needed the ego's thoughts to live our life, and therefore freedom from suffering is possible.

YOUR EXPERIENCE IS THE RIGHT EXPERIENCE

The ego is always looking for a better experience—the right experience. The truth is you are already having the right experience and have always been! What if you really knew that to be true? Just take that in for a moment: The experience you are having right now is exactly the right experience. It's the experience you *should* be having. This truth counteracts the ego's insistence that the present moment *should* be different. The present moment shouldn't be different!

LIFE IS ABOUT SOMETHING MUCH MORE PROFOUND THAN FULFILLING THE EGO'S DESIRES

The ego wants life to serve *it,* but life doesn't do that very well because it serves a higher purpose: the evolution of the Whole. No wonder the ego doesn't trust life to serve it—because life doesn't serve it! When we expect life to be the way it is—unpredictable, changeable, challenging, and full of growth—then life is absolutely trustworthy. Essence has designed life to be this way, so Essence has no problem with life being this way. The ego distrusts life only because it doesn't accept that life is not about fulfilling the ego's desires and dreams, but about something much more profound and wonderful. Life is about evolution and, more specifically, about our evolution toward love and away from fear. For providing that evolution, life is totally trustworthy.

FALL IN LOVE WITH THE UNKNOWN

We have always been living in the unknown, but we pretend to know because the mind prefers that to not knowing. We don't know what is going to happen tomorrow or what we will do, but we pretend to. We decide to do something, and that makes us feel like we know what we will do, but we still don't know for certain if we will do that. How many times have you said you were going to do something and then suddenly changed your mind? Instead of being afraid of not knowing, you have to fall in love with it.

GIVE YOUR ATTENTION TO WHAT YOU ARE EXPERIENCING, NOT TO YOUR RESISTANCE TO LIFE

To love what we are experiencing, all it takes is our attention. When we give our attention to something, love flows to it. So if you want to love what you are experiencing instead of resist it, give it your attention. That is the antidote to the ego's resistance. If we give our attention to our resistance, we are loving resisting. Then resistance is magnified and becomes our experience. Because the ego doesn't want to love, we have to find within us that which is willing to love life just as it is. We have to summon that to counter the ego's complaints and resistance to life. We summon, or align with, Essence by giving our full attention to the Now.

YOU ARE FAR GRANDER THAN YOU EVER IMAGINED

We are far more precious than we may imagine. We are not the petty voice of the ego. The true self is hidden by the false one. Waking up to the truth only requires accepting the possibility that you are far grander than you have ever imagined. Our imagination of who we are leads us astray. We are not any of our self-images, but beyond all images and all thoughts. We are the space in which thought emerges and the space in between the thoughts. This silence in between the thoughts is golden because, like gold, it's precious, pure, eternal, and true, unlike thoughts, which are evanescent and of little value. By simply putting your attention on silence, you become it. Everything stills, and there you are!

DON'T LET FEAR KEEP YOU HOSTAGE

Fear is what keeps people identified with the ego. It keeps people hostage to the suffering inherent in the human condition, but it doesn't have to be that way. Fear is the most powerful tool the ego has, but fear is just a thought. And how powerful is a thought, really? If you don't believe a thought, it has no power whatsoever. Fear is only powerful if you believe it, and it has no other ability to affect reality. The catch is that fear is so believable. A fearful thought, which is always a thought about the future, gets cloaked in emotions, and those emotions are felt in the body, making the fear seem very real. You interpret that feeling as meaningful: If you feel something that strongly, you assume the thought must be meaningful. You think there must be something true about that fearful thought, so you believe it and give it the power to affect your life.

FALL INTO THE SILENCE IN BETWEEN THOUGHTS

When you put your attention on the spaciousness that you are or on the silence in between the thoughts, you fall into that spaciousness. You become it, if even for just a brief second. The more you notice that space, or spaciousness, the more familiar you become with it, and the more you are able to see the truth about it—that it is who you are. This silent, all-accepting conscious space is what you and everyone and everything else emanate from. Consciousness is what you are.

YOU ARE RESPONSIBLE FOR HOW YOU INTERPRET YOUR EXPERIENCE

The present moment shouldn't be different! It has been co-created by you, the Oneness, and everything else that exists in creation. Life is a miraculous dance with not only you, but also everything that has brought you to the present moment. You are part of a greater Whole, and you move within that Whole, but not on your own. You move in response to everything in the Whole, and everything else does too. You aren't responsible for what is arising in the moment; you are only responsible for your interpretation of it. That is where your power lies and your choice.

SEE THE TRUTH ABOUT YOUR DESIRES

Desires don't cause suffering. Desires come and go. They arise in the mind and then disappear. If that were all that happened, there would be no suffering. However, something else happens: attachment. Attachment happens as a result of a story we tell ourselves about a desire: "I will be happy when...." Desire is a drive, an impulse, that comes and goes; attachment gives that impulse fuel and makes it burn: "I want this because...." Thus, the story is born. The general story is that fulfilling our desires will make us happy and not doing so will make us unhappy.

LOVE IT OR HATE IT, BUT YOU STILL HAVE JUST THIS MOMENT

It all boils down to *now,* this moment. The experience you are having right now is it. The present moment is life—it's what is real. And the moment is just what it is. You can pile all the thoughts, feelings, and imaginations that you want into this moment, but it is still just this. And no matter how much or how little money you have, how youthful or old you are, how talented or untalented you are, how successful or unsuccessful you are, you still have just this moment. No billionaire has any more or less of this moment. People try to dress the moment up in ideas, but it still comes down to just this simple moment. You can love it or hate it, but you still just have this moment.

TRUST ESSENCE OR TRUST THE EGO

There are two possibilities: trusting the ego or trusting Essence. There isn't anything else here to trust. In any moment, we are trusting either the ego or Essence. Most people are trusting their egoic minds, not Essence, but even they respond to Essence some of the time. Whatever we give our attention to is what we are loving and trusting, and for most people, that is the egoic mind. What makes life so difficult to trust is that the ego doesn't trust life. So if we are trusting the ego, we won't trust life.

NOTICE THE ALIVENESS

When we are in our body and senses and not in our head, or mind, we experience a sense of aliveness that is felt as a subtle energetic vibration, or tingling, and a sense of being alive, illumined, and aware. This is how who we really are is experienced by the body-mind. This aliveness is the felt-sense of who we really are and what we experience when we are in the Now. When we are aligned with who we really are and not identified with the ego, we feel this aliveness, this beingness, this Presence energetically, and it is very pleasurable. The fact that who we really are, Essence, can be felt energetically is very handy because this makes identifying when we are aligned with Essence and when we aren't easier. The sense of aliveness can also help us realign with Essence when we are identified with the ego: If you find yourself contracted and suffering, you can search for the sense of aliveness, which is always present, and focus on it.

DO WHAT MAKES YOU HAPPY

When you are doing your life purpose, you know it because of how it feels: You feel happy. Life feels good, and you feel good about yourself. What others may feel about what you are doing doesn't matter because you feel good about it. There is a surety, a certainty, about your course and a confidence and commitment that goes with that, which tends to inspire the respect and support of others.

WHAT ARE YOU GIVING YOUR
ATTENTION TO?

Giving attention is a very basic form of love and a way that love can be expressed very simply in the world. What you give your attention to is what you love. If you are giving your attention to the egoic mind, then you are loving that and joining with that. If you are giving your attention to others, then you are loving them and joining with them. Asking yourself, "What am I giving my attention to?" can be an excellent spiritual practice, and it will help you train yourself away from the habit of identifying with the egoic mind.

STRESS IS A SIGN YOU ARE BELIEVING THE MIND

Stress is a sign that we need to stop a moment and examine what we are saying to ourselves. It is created by a negative thought about what we are doing or about something else, such as the past or the future, a judgment, or a *should*. Not being present to what we are doing but, instead, being identified with our thoughts about what we are doing or about something else causes stress because most thoughts generated by the ego are negative. Negativity causes the contraction in our body and in our energy that we call stress.

CHOOSE ESSENCE INSTEAD OF THE EGO

Choosing Essence is simply a matter of putting our attention on Essence's qualities—love, peace, joy, acceptance, gratitude, and contentment—instead of on the ego (the *I*), its thoughts, desires, fantasies, beliefs, opinions, and on the feelings that arise from them.

WHAT IS IT THAT IS AWARE OF THOUGHTS?

When we are identified with the egoic mind, we believe we are who we think we are: our self-image and the labels we have for ourselves. But is that who you are? If that is who you are, then who is it that is able to think about this question? What is it that is aware of the ideas that make up your self-image? What is it that is aware of the coming and going of thoughts? This idea *me* may seem to reside in the body or the mind or both, but what is it that is aware of the body and the mind? Could that be who you are, and the body and the mind are just functioning within that awareness? In that case, would you be limited to just the body and mind, or could you actually be anything you are aware of right now? Could all of it be you? What if that were true? What would that mean? Life would be lived from a very different place. These questions can wake you up out of the egoic state of consciousness.

WHO ARE YOU?

You can be the richest person in the universe or the poorest, but without the story "I'm the richest/poorest person in the universe," who are you? In this moment, without all your stories and self-images, who or what are you? You are just this that is having an experience of the present moment. The miracle is that *this* is the same in every individual. This that you are is what everyone else is too. Our ideas and self-images create a false identity, a costume, that we wear and bring into the moment, which colors our experience of it. When thoughts are stripped away, all we have left is life living itself *now*, and that's all that has ever been going on.

WHAT IF YOU BELIEVED IN THE HEART AS MUCH AS YOU BELIEVE THE EGO?

Trusting the Heart may seem difficult, but once you see how untrustworthy what you have been trusting actually is, trusting the Heart becomes much easier. Has following your Heart ever failed you? Everyone has had experiences of following the Heart. What happened when you did? Yes, it was probably scary (and exhilarating), and doing so didn't mean everything went smoothly and exactly as your ego wanted (Does it ever?). But what we discover when we follow our Heart is that the challenges we meet are rich, and the resources we need to deal with them show up. Following the ego's desires and plans by no means guarantees getting what the ego wants either; it's only the *belief* that following the ego's plans will get us what we want that makes trusting the ego easier. What if you believed in the Heart as much as you believe in the ego?

GIVE UP THE DRAMA

A part of us doesn't want to experience life purely and simply—the ego. It wouldn't exist without the mental drama it creates. It exists and thrives on thoughts about the past and plans of the future. It constantly mulls over the story of *me:* "How's it going for me?" "How am I going to do?" "How did I do?" "What do I have to do to get things to go my way?" Evaluations and plans are the stuff the ego feeds on, which cause it to loom large in our consciousness, blocking out awareness of other aspects of reality. When we live in the egoic state of consciousness, life is about the story and how it's going, and all the worries, fears, concerns, and problems entailed in that. That is the ongoing drama the ego is engrossed in. However, there is another life living itself under or behind or beyond all of that, and that is reality.

LET EVERYTHING BE THE WAY IT IS

We think we have to like something to accept it, but accepting something just means letting it be the way it is. It is our rejection of what is happening that causes us to suffer. The ego resists loss and difficulties with all its might because the ego fears challenges. The ego's fear turns a challenging experience into something that's hard to bear. Fear takes us out of the moment and into the ego's world, where dreams just as easily become nightmares. The truth is, even in the most challenging moments, love, peace, joy, acceptance, and excitement about life are present, at least subtly. These positive feeling states co-exist with the pain, sadness, anger, and fear the ego produces. During difficult times, we are challenged to discover these positive feeling states instead of following the ego into its world.

EXPERIENCE YOUR NOBODY-NESS AND
YOUR EVERYBODY-NESS

When we drop out of our mind and into the moment and into our Heart, we experience who we really are, but not as an image. When we are in the Heart (Essence), images and ideas drop away, and what is left is simply an experience of being, or of being nobody in particular: not a male or female, not young or old, not attractive or unattractive, not smart or dumb, not anything we can name. The experience of our true nature is an experience of emptiness. Our true nature is empty of all definition; and yet, it is full and complete, lacking nothing. This experience of being nobody and nothing is equally an experience of being everybody and everything because this emptiness is without boundaries and therefore includes everything; nothing is left out. There's no me and you, but only spaciousness, beingness. This unending spaciousness is who we are.

YOU ARE WHAT LOOKS

When we experience ourselves looking out of our eyes, we experience our body very differently than when we imagine our body or when we see it in a mirror. Stop a moment and just look at the miracle that is your body, without any comments or thoughts about it. What do you experience? You are likely to experience the body as something apart from yourself, something you look upon with amazement. Whose hand is that? Whose leg is that? The body appears to be more of a vehicle for who you are than who you are. And so it is. The body is a vehicle for who we really are. The mind pretends that this vehicle *is* who we are, but the body is only a temporary carrier for the consciousness that is looking out of our eyes.

DO WHAT ESSENCE LOVES

If there is any activity we do too much of to the detriment of Essence, it's thinking. What if some of the activities that Essence loves—creating, dancing, singing, walking in nature, exploring, just being, and meditating—replaced some of that thinking? This would dramatically change your world because you would be living more in Essence and less in the ego. What a different life that would be. Would it be so hard to do more of what Essence loves? What would you really lose in exchange for some joy? What really matters to you?

DON'T DRAG THE PAST INTO THE PRESENT

Nothing can change the past, including thought. However, dwelling on thoughts about the past does change our experience of the Now. When we drag the past into the present, everything else that belongs to the Now is marginalized and overlooked. All we see is the past or, more accurately, our story about it. All we can ever have of the past is our story about it, and that story is very unsatisfying. Our stories about the past don't feed our soul like the Now does. And worse, any story is usually a sad tale that keeps us caught up in negative feelings, and then those feelings become our current experience of life.

NOTICE THAT YOU ARE AWARE

Becoming aware of ourselves as Awareness is as easy as noticing we are aware. Awareness is so obvious that it's taken for granted, overlooked. Yet, when we turn our attention to what is aware, we get a glimpse of the mysteriousness of who we really are. What is it that seems to be looking out of your eyes and taking in the world? What is looking isn't your eyes. Our eyes are an instrument of awareness, but awareness isn't located inside our head or body, although it seems to be. It is more like awareness is funneled through the body-mind.

YOU ARE WHAT IS CONSCIOUS OF LIFE

Awareness always is. There is never a time when we are not aware. Even when we sleep and dream, we are aware we have slept and dreamt. Awareness is the one constant in life. It is even constant after this life, for awareness—consciousness—continues even after the body has died, although after death, consciousness is no longer connected to the body. We are what is conscious of life and conscious of everything coming and going. When our attention is placed on this consciousness rather than on the comings and goings in life, we feel at peace with whatever is coming and going.

STOP RESPONDING TO YOUR THOUGHTS

The biggest challenge to being aligned with Essence and in the flow is being identified with thought. Thinking is not actually the problem, but our relationship to it, whether we are identified with it and believe it or not. Thoughts will always arise in the mind, and not all of them are a problem; some are inspired by Essence. However, most thoughts represent the programming we were given, which maintains the sense of *I* and the egoic state of consciousness. Most thoughts are superfluous to living and only interfere with happiness. Being aware of our thoughts is the antidote to identifying with them. We don't have to stop thinking or do away with our negative thoughts to be happy and aligned with Essence; we only have to stop responding to them.

NOTICE WHAT IS ALIVE

What gives your body life? That is who you are. You are what brings life into the body and sustains it through breathing it and enlivening every system. Who we are is the consciousness that allows the body to be alive and aware. The more we notice this Awareness, the stronger the energetic experience that accompanies Awareness becomes. This energetic experience is an experience of aliveness. So although who we really are isn't physical, it can be sensed physically, and it is sensed as vibrational energy, a feeling of aliveness. The energetic sense of aliveness is as close as we can get to experiencing who we really are physically. Becoming more aware of this subtle vibration, this aliveness, helps us align with our true nature.

SEE THE TRUTH ABOUT YOUR FANTASIES

Having a fantasy is actually more painful than it is pleasurable because the pleasure lasts only momentarily, while the pain of not having what we want can interfere with experiencing and appreciating what we do have in this moment. It is sad indeed to miss this moment because of a fantasy, especially when that fantasy floods the moment with the pain of incompletion, frustration, worry, fear, anger, and sadness. These are the real fruits of fantasizing. Fantasy not only takes us out of the moment, which is actually full of everything we need and are looking for to be happy, but also fosters a secondary, or false, reality that results in painful thoughts and emotions. Fantasizing may seem pleasurable, fun, and harmless, but the short-lived pleasure and fun actually come at a high price.

GO TOWARDS JOY, PEACE, AND LOVE

Essence doesn't produce emotions, but Essence is experienced as feelings of joy, elation, peace, contentment, acceptance, love, patience, wisdom, and compassion. Essence steers us toward its intentions with these feelings and away from what is not compatible with our life plan with a sense of no or with feelings of sadness. Essence's guidance rarely shows up as words in the mind, but when it does, those words ring true, and we feel expansive and joyful, which is quite different from how most thoughts make us feel.

DON'T LET THOUGHTS AND FEELINGS COLOR THE NOW

Thoughts create an alternate reality, a subplot to the Now, and people get lost in this pretend subplot and don't notice other things about the Now. When we bring this alternate reality into the Now, it changes our experience of the Now. It colors it. We no longer experience the Now purely but through the lens of our egoic mind, which is the generator of thoughts and feelings. Our thoughts and feelings come and go in the Now, but unlike other things that come and go in the Now, such as sights and sounds, thoughts and feelings, when we identify with them, change our *experience* of the Now. If we aren't identified with a thought or feeling, we will feel the peace and contentment of the Now. If we are identified with a thought or feeling, we will feel anxious, restless, discontent, and possibly some other negative feelings.

LOOK OUTSIDE THE MIND FOR TRUE HAPPINESS AND TRUE GUIDANCE

When we are in the moment without giving our full attention to our thoughts, as we usually do, we discover that many things are part of the Now besides thoughts. The ego discounts these other things as unimportant and uninteresting. If we pay attention to the ego, we won't have a chance to find out about these other things for ourselves. When we finally become disillusioned with the egoic mind's complaints, judgments, poor guidance, and version of reality, we begin to look outside the mind for true happiness and wiser guidance.

MAKE LISTENING A SPIRITUAL PRACTICE

You can make listening a spiritual practice by just listening without thinking. You can't listen and think at the same time, so if you catch yourself thinking, just bring yourself back to listening. Any judgments, opinions, stories, beliefs, labels, or concepts that arise while you are listening are the mind coming in. Note these and then return to listening. Just keep coming back to listening and see how this transforms your life.

BECOME AWARE OF WHAT IS AWARE

The process of spiritual awakening, or realization of your true self, is a process of becoming aware of yourself as Awareness. The course of spiritual evolution is a gradual dis-identification with the false self, or the ego, and that which flows from it— thoughts, beliefs, opinions, judgments, desires, feelings, memories, hopes, and fantasies—and a reunification with the spiritual self, or Essence, that which you truly are, which is devoid of those mental constructs.

DO THIS SIMPLE MEDITATION
THROUGHOUT YOUR DAY

Meditation is as simple as just noticing, or being aware of, what is coming into your senses, what thoughts and feelings are arising, what intuitions or inspirations are arising, what motivations and urges are arising, and what energetic sensations are being experienced without getting involved in the mind's commentary about these. Notice not only what is coming in through your senses, but also the impact it has on you subtly and not so subtly. The goal of meditation is to experience your true nature, or Essence, and Essence is this noticing, aware Presence that you imitate when you sit down to meditate. In imitating Awareness by being aware of everything you are experiencing in the moment, but not identifying with it, you become that Awareness; you drop into it. Noticing without getting involved in any mental commentary or thoughts about what you are noticing aligns you with Essence.

FIND YOUR WAY HOME BY JUST BEING

We look for the sense of being Home in a physical home, in a family, in a lover. But unless we can experience it in the still moments of our life, no house, family, lover, or anything else will ever satisfy our longing for Home. The feeling of being Home is never found by doing, going somewhere, having things, or thinking, but by simply stopping and just *being* long enough to let ourselves feel that we are Home. Our longing for Home can call it forth. Know Home, value it, want it, and you will have it. The most precious attainment is right here in Stillness and in just being.

DON'T LET DISSATISFACTION RUIN
THIS PERFECTION

The ego is always trying to improve on the present moment, but instead, it ruins it with its dissatisfaction. It tells you the present moment would be better if…. (Fill in the blank: I were richer, prettier, thinner, more successful, in a relationship, not in a relationship, etc.) That's a lie. None of those things changes your experience of the present moment unless you believe that lie. If you believe that lie, you won't enjoy the moment. You won't really let yourself fully experience it. If you don't believe that lie, you discover that you have everything you need to be happy.

DON'T MISTAKE THE EGOIC MIND FOR A FRIEND

The truth is the egoic mind has nothing of value for us, not even as a friend or companion. If we continue to hold friendly conversations with it in our head, we will continue to live in our head rather than in the Now, where communications from Essence are received. Holding chats with the egoic mind may seem harmless, but it strengthens the ego and alienates us from life and Essence, which needs our cooperation to unfold life according to its plan and intentions. Chatting with the mind passes the time, like chatting with any friend, but being involved with the mind this way won't bring fulfillment or lead to happiness. This friend is not a wise friend, and conversing with it is a waste of time and energy. Once we really see this, we can begin living from a deeper and richer place, a place where joy, contentment, and peace are possible.

LET GO OF THOUGHTS ABOUT THE PAST

Letting go seems so difficult at times, but whatever we are trying to let go of is already gone. It's in the past, and life has moved on and is bringing us other things. All that is ever really left to let go of are our thoughts about something in the past. Letting go naturally happens when we are just here right now, in the moment. The Now is free of the past, unless we bring the past into the Now through thought. Thought is the only thing that can disturb the peace and contentment of the Now. Even a shocking event is here only briefly and then gone. The only way a terrible event lives on is through thoughts about it.

DON'T BELIEVE YOUR NEGATIVE BELIEFS

Your negative beliefs are powerful if you believe them. But if you don't, they have no power whatsoever. Can an idea affect the world? Only if it's believed and only if it's put into action. The belief itself, which is just an idea, has no power of its own. Everyone has beliefs and negative thoughts. If they aren't believed, they end there and quickly disappear. They may show up again and again, but if they are ignored, they don't affect you or anything else. You don't have the power to determine what thoughts show up in your mind, but you do have the power to choose to believe them and respond to them or not.

RESIST THE PATH OF LEAST RESISTANCE—THE EGO

No wonder we feel resistance when we listen to the egoic mind. Not only is the ego's nature to resist, but what it says is also often in conflict with Essence. In that case, resisting is good if what you are resisting is the ego. By all means resist unkindness, resist judgment, resist hatred, resist selfishness, resist false beliefs, resist the path of least resistance. Choosing to resist the ego's selfishness and bullying tactics will bring you into alignment with Essence.

DON'T MAKE DIFFERENCES INTO A PROBLEM

Although differences often result in conflict and disharmony in relationships, they don't have to. So what if your mind doesn't like something? You are not your mind, and when you know that, what the mind says isn't a problem. It's only when you are identified with the mind ("I think it, therefore it's true") that differences become a problem because then we believe what comes next: the mind's assertion of what needs to be done about that difference. That's where differences become a problem: We believe the mind's solution to the "problem" of differences.

DESIRE WHAT IS HERE NOW

We long for what we don't have because we believe that having it will finally bring us peace and happiness. We don't realize that the lack of peace and happiness we are feeling is actually a result of desiring what we don't have. The desire is the *cause* of our unhappiness, not the fact that the desire is unfulfilled. When we examine desire more closely, the truth about it becomes obvious. Desire is painful. We suffer because we believe we are lacking something necessary for our happiness. That's a very sad (and untrue!) story, but this story is essentially everyone's story. Everyone feels this way because the mind is programmed to be unhappy with whatever is happening. The ego refuses to be happy because if it didn't come up with reasons to be unhappy, it would be out of a job, since the ego is in the business of problem-creation and problem-solving.

GIVE UP YOUR STORIES

When you are in the flow, you experience whatever you are experiencing without telling a story about it. Thoughts may arise, but you recognize them as thoughts, as an attempt on the part of the ego to define the moment because that is what it tries to do. Meanwhile, you just stay in the experience of the moment, which is forever changing into something else. When you are in the flow, you know yourself as that which is aware of the thoughts, not someone who is thinking them.

SAY YES TO IT ALL

When we drop out of the egoic mind and into Essence, we experience Essence's joy in this Mystery. This joy is ongoing, no matter what experience Essence is having. It doesn't reject any experience, but says yes to it all. Every experience is welcome and valuable to Essence. It exists to have experience, and any experience will do!

UNHAPPINESS IS ONLY CAUSED BY THOUGHTS

Whenever we identify with our thoughts—any thought—we lose touch with the peace and contentment of the Now. We often think that whatever is happening is making us unhappy, but what we are bringing into the peaceful moment through thought is what is making us unhappy. Once you realize the result of bringing thoughts into the Now, you can choose to not give your attention to your thoughts. Notice how you immediately relax when you give your attention to what is present right here and now instead of to your thoughts and feelings.

WHAT DO YOU BELIEVE IS MISSING NOW?

What do you believe is missing now? Take a moment to answer this question. This is the source of any suffering you may be feeling. What if you didn't believe you needed that to be happy, safe, or secure? Without that belief, you would drop into Essence, which experiences life as a blessing—and as trustworthy. Life provides what we need, although what it provides may not always be what the ego wants. Providing everyone with what their egos want would be impossible. What would a world like that look like? The Intelligence that we are provides each of us with what is necessary for the Whole to evolve and expand.

THE EGO HAS IT BACKWARDS

Life itself is benign, but the ego makes life feel threatening or, at best, dull. The ego is either fending off its perceived difficulties and problems or trying to drum up some excitement, drama, and specialness. It doesn't know how to play the game of life simply; it opts for trouble and drama. But drama doesn't equal happiness, and simplicity and peace don't equal boredom. The ego has it backwards. It tries to create a happy life, and all it does is take us away from happiness.

YOUR THOUGHTS ARE NOT YOURS

To free ourselves from the egoic mind, all we have to do is notice the impact our thoughts have on our experience of life. Does the experience you are having cause you to contract and feel bad, or does a thought about the experience cause this contraction? This distinction is a big one. Once we see that it is only our thoughts that cause us to feel contracted and tense, we can become free from those thoughts. The only thing that keeps us tied to our thoughts, or imprisoned by them, is the belief that our thoughts belong to us and are therefore valid and necessary. They are not "your" thoughts, and they are not valid or necessary. When we finally see this, what a revelation that is, and so obvious really.

CHOOSE YOUR EXPERIENCE OF THE MOMENT

There are two possible experiences of every moment: the moment as experienced by Essence and the moment as experienced by the ego. The ego's experience of the moment is struggle, conflict, effort, dissatisfaction, restlessness, and unease. Essence's experience of it is freedom, happiness, peace, acceptance, contentment, and joy. Either experience is possible in any moment, depending on whether we are identified with the ego or with Essence.

THE ONLY PROBLEM IS THAT THE EGO DOESN'T LIKE SOMETHING

The ego is what labels anything it doesn't like or desire as a problem, when really the only problem is that the ego doesn't like or desire it. Essence doesn't have a problem with anything that is happening because it doesn't have a judgment, opinion, desire, or story about it. Judgments, opinions, desires, and stories are the spin the ego gives to experience, which causes the ego to resist life and consequently to suffer. To Essence, every experience is valuable and appreciated because, for Essence, experience is the purpose of life.

THOUGHTS ARE NOT NECESSARY

How many of the thoughts you are having right now, or in any other moment, actually contribute to what you are doing and experiencing? When you examine this, you discover that most thoughts don't contribute to your life, and they aren't needed to function. Try to find an example of a thought that is necessary. Necessary thoughts are few and far between. Isn't it funny how important and necessary we think thinking is? This is part of the grand illusion. We think we need to think to make life happen and make it go smoothly. But when we start examining the contribution that our thoughts make to each moment—to our experience and to whatever we are doing—we discover that thoughts are not only unnecessary, but also clutter the moment with confusion, negativity, and stress and therefore interfere with what we are experiencing and doing— and with our happiness.

THERE'S ONLY SO MUCH YOU CAN DO NOW

Life is never actually overwhelming because there's only so much we can do in a moment. But the mind brings ideas into the present moment about what we "have" to do, what we want to do, what we've done in the past, what others want us to do, whether we are able to do something, and ideas about any number of other things that are unrelated to what we are doing or need to do. All these thoughts confuse and stress us out. They are unnecessary and counterproductive. Stress makes us less effective and efficient, it makes us crabby and unhappy, and it is unhealthy. Those are the real results of giving our attention to thoughts and letting them guide our life.

YOUR "PRINCE" IS ALREADY HERE

We want to know the future because we want confirmation of the ego's belief that the present is flawed and that it will be redeemed by something better in the future. We want someone to tell us "Yes, your prince (princess) will come and you will live happily ever after." The ego's basic stance is that what is happening now isn't good enough, but someday it will be, and that will last forever. It is a fairytale that is so deeply embedded in our makeup that we don't even realize we are telling ourselves this. When you find yourself wanting a better moment—wanting something else in the future—it can be helpful to ask: What will that give me? We think we will finally be happy when that moment arrives. What we discover when we do get what we want is that even that wonderful moment disappears. Life keeps moving on, bringing us a mixture of what we like and don't like. Why not like—love—it all because it won't be here for long, it will never be this way again, and it's all you've got.

EXPERIENCE IS NEITHER GOOD NOR BAD

We assume any discontentment we feel is the result of something wrong with or missing in our life. We don't realize our unhappiness comes from taking on the ego's viewpoint. Life just is the way it is, neither good nor bad really. An experience or a situation is the way it is, and that will soon change. Why make it wrong? Nevertheless, dissatisfaction is the ongoing state of the ego, and when we are identified with it, we feel unhappy. Every moment becomes something to complain about, and these complaints fuel actions, many of which are a waste of energy, except from the ego's point of view.

LOVE WHATEVER IS

Essence loves whatever is happening because it either created it or allowed you (your ego) to create it for your growth and evolution. What you learn to love about whatever you are experiencing is not how it makes you feel, but how perfectly it is suited to support your evolution toward greater love, wisdom, compassion, courage, patience, and understanding. Life is perfectly designed to evolve us, and that is what is lovable about every moment.

NOTICE THE EFFECT OF YOUR THOUGHTS

The more we notice the effect that paying attention to our thoughts has on us—contraction, stress, tension, unhappiness, and negative feelings—the more we will choose to turn our attention away from the world of thought and onto this simple moment. The Now is full and rich and has all the peace we have ever wanted. What the Now doesn't have are the problems and drama created by the ego, which the ego wants because problems and drama keep us attached to our thoughts. Are you ready to exchange your problems and the ego's drama for peace, contentment, and the experience of being nobody? It's a really good deal.

ACCEPT THE GIFT OF THIS PERFECT MOMENT

You need nothing more than the experience you are having right now. It is enough. It is plenty. It is perfect just as it is. It was designed for you, given to you for your experience. All you have to do, and all you have ever had to do is accept this gift. Take it and let it in. Let yourself experience the present moment just as it is. It doesn't get any better than this. That is the simple truth the ego refuses to accept, and it will suffer as long as that is the case.

WITNESS THE MIND

Learning to witness your mind is the first step in becoming free of the ego and its conditioning. But to free ourselves from identification with the egoic mind takes more than just witnessing the mind. If you witness your mind and still believe it, you are not any freer than when you were identified with it. To be free of our conditioning, we also have to see the falseness of it. Even so, there's one more very important step. Many people are aware of their egoic mind and the falseness of it, but they still aren't free of it because they are still giving their attention to it. The experience is like watching a bad TV show, acknowledging that it is bad, but staying glued to the TV set. Until you put your attention on what is true rather than on what is false, you won't be free. You will still be experiencing your ego more than your true self.

IGNORE NEGATIVE AND IRRELEVANT THOUGHTS

Every time you successfully ignore a negative or irrelevant thought, which is most thoughts, it becomes easier. Irrelevant or unnecessary thoughts are much easier to ignore than negative ones because negative thoughts are entangled with our identity. Irrelevant or unnecessary thoughts are any thoughts that don't actually serve our functioning in the moment. Notice how often your egoic mind just chatters about irrelevant things, including the past and future. You can easily see that you don't need thoughts about the past and future to function in the moment. So to start with, try ignoring all of those thoughts. This practice will also get you used to noticing what your mind is up to. You will discover how unnecessary or negative most of what you think is. This can be very enlightening!

DON'T WASTE TIME ON THOUGHTS ABOUT LIFE

Primarily, the experience of any moment is a sensory one if we aren't identified with the stories the mind brings into the moment, which create suffering. This emotional suffering doesn't have to be part of any moment. Suffering is caused by the egoic mind, by thoughts *about* life, not by life. If we are just in the Now, the ups and downs of life don't affect us because we aren't bringing the story of the "up" or "down" into the present moment. All we have is the present moment and what is showing up *now*.

NOTICE THAT HAPPINESS IS HERE

Happiness isn't something to attain or achieve but something to notice. If you are busy trying to achieve happiness, you are probably overlooking it. The ego tries to get happiness from doing, having, or being someone, while the spiritual ego tries to get it from transcending all of that. For the ego, spiritual freedom, or enlightenment, is just another thing to be achieved. Wanting happiness and freedom from the suffering of the ego are worthwhile desires. The problem is that wanting anything implies you don't already have it. You *believe* you aren't free when you already are. You *believe* you need to do something to be happy, and you don't. This truth is very difficult for the ego to grasp. The ego doesn't notice the happiness that is already present in the moment because that happiness doesn't look like the ego imagines or wants happiness to look.

YOU ARE ALREADY HOME

What a surprise it is to discover that you have never needed to strive to survive and be happy after all. Like Dorothy in *The Wizard of Oz*, who discovered that she always had the means for going home, you already have what you need to be happy and safe. You have never really left Home. However, if you don't believe you already have what you need to be happy and safe, it is as if it isn't true: If we don't know the ruby slippers will take us home, it's like not having them. The ego keeps us from seeing the truth about those ruby slippers—it keeps us from seeing the truth about life. Home is right here, right now, but we may not realize it and therefore not experience Home, or Essence, as much as we might.

FIND WHAT'S HERE THAT ISN'T HAVING A PROBLEM

Once you realize you aren't the mind that is having a problem with life, then—guess what!—you don't have a problem anymore. There is something else present that isn't having a problem with life, and that is what, or who, you really are. When we align with that, we can be happy and stress-free regardless of what is going on.

THE EGO'S DREAM OF HAPPINESS IS UNATTAINABLE

When true happiness shows up, the ego is bored with it: It's too plain, too ordinary, and it doesn't leave us feeling special or above the fray. It doesn't take away our problems, which is the ego's idea of happiness. The ego wants no more difficulties: no more sickness, no more need for money, no more work, no more bad feelings, only unending pleasure and bliss. Such perfection is the ego's idea of a successful life. However, the happiness the ego dreams of will never be attained by anyone. The ego denies the reality of this dimension, where challenges are necessary to evolution and blissful states and pleasures come and go.

MAKE ROOM FOR PEACE

We can make room for more experiences of radiance, peace, and beauty; and when we do, they arrive. When we make an intention to experience peace, when we value it enough to make room for it and invite it into our busy lives, it arrives bearing gifts. We make room for this guest, not by *doing* anything, but by just being, just allowing ourselves to rest, once and for all, in this sweet moment with no agenda, no purpose, no reason but to just experience the moment as it is. We make room for peace and happiness by just noticing them. We notice that they are already here, and noticing them brings them more strongly into focus. Peace and happiness are always here, but they often go unnoticed.

SEE WHAT HAPPENS NEXT AND WHAT ESSENCE MOVES YOU TO DO

Suffering is a choice: We can have our story of *me,* or we can just be alive in the present moment and see what happens next and what Essence moves us to do. Life springs out of the Now. We can trust life to do that. Life doesn't need the ego's agenda or its desires for life to happen. When we drop into the Now, we experience the life we are having, without trying to make it be any different than it is. When we are in the Now, we gain everything we have been looking for: peace, contentment, happiness, and love. From the Now, life takes care of itself because we are Life.

WHAT DO YOU REALLY WANT?

What does matter most to you? What do you really want? This is a very important question. It's fine if what matters to you is getting what the ego wants. Sometime, in this lifetime or in another, that will change. Just be clear that awakening is not a way—a more spiritual way—of getting what the ego wants. Awakening is the realization that what the ego wants is irrelevant to this life and to our happiness. What does Essence want? That is the question. What is the deepest desire of your soul for this lifetime and for this moment?

GIVING LOVE IS THE SECRET TO EXPERIENCING IT

We are free to choose the ego's way and withhold what we have to give or to give more freely. The result of these two choices is very different: When we give freely, we feel full and complete; when we withhold, we feel small, petty, impotent, and lacking. We are meant to learn this great truth, that giving ful-fills us, while withholding and trying to get causes us to feel empty and even more needy. This truth runs counter to our programming, which drives us to try to get something from others to fulfill our neediness, only to end up even more needy, grasping, lacking, and unfulfilled.

DO WHAT'S IN FRONT OF YOU

Living from Essence is often a matter of doing what is in front of us: If something needs picking up, you naturally pick it up. If someone shows up who needs help, you offer it. If dishes need washing, you wash the dishes. If a job needs to be done, you do it, one step at a time. Or if you need to rest, you rest. Or if you need to eat, you eat. The mind complicates life with a lot of thoughts about how, when, why and whether to do various things. It plans and thinks about doing things, when life is simpler than that. Much of the time, living is just a matter of doing what arises to be done.

THERE IS NO TIME BUT THE PRESENT

With its thoughts about the past and future, the egoic mind creates a sense of time and then causes us to feel there isn't enough time. The ego is a time tyrant. Being in the present, on the other hand, without the mind's tyranny, is a timeless place of enjoying whatever we are doing, no matter what it is. Since we can only get so much done in any moment, we might as well enjoy what we are doing. Listening to the egoic mind doesn't help us accomplish more; it only makes us feel inadequate, stressed, and discontent with whatever we are doing.

MAKE THE MOST OF LIFE

We are all so powerful. We have the power to make the most out of life, out of the moment, or to make life unpleasant. The moment is what it is, and what we bring to the moment makes it either enjoyable or stressful and unpleasant. We are meant to discover that we are powerful creators, if not of our entire reality, at least of our *experience* of reality. We aren't responsible for what each moment holds, but we are responsible for our experience of each moment because we have the power to make any moment heaven or hell. We don't create our entire reality, since other forces are at work, but how we interact with and think about reality (what's showing up in the moment) affects it to some extent and, surely, affects our experience of it.

SQUEEZE THE MOST OUT OF THE MOMENT

How much enjoyment can you squeeze out of the present moment? What if that was your job, your aim, your sole (or soul's) purpose? If you were determined to get enjoyment out of every moment, you would learn to do whatever it took. What it takes is not listening to negative thoughts, yours or anyone else's. Disregarding negative thoughts isn't hiding our head in the sand, but simply not allowing the negative to clutter and influence our experience of the present moment. The moment is never helped or improved by negativity, although we are programmed to think our negative thoughts, worries, and fears serve a useful function. When you really examine this idea, however, you see that negativity doesn't serve. Focusing on negativity and fears doesn't make anyone a better person, nor does doing that help us function better in the world. In fact, the truth is quite the opposite.

BE IN JOY

Enjoying life is a matter of recognizing that which is "in joy," which is the Being that we are: Essence. The Being that is living our life is rejoicing in the experience it is having, regardless of what that experience is, because this Being has no judgments or stories to tell about any experience or anything. It is just "in joy" all the time. We have the power to experience this joy or to disregard it and, instead, experience our mind's stories and judgments about the moment, our mind's endless commentary. We are powerful enough to recognize which choice brings more joy, and we are powerful enough to be able to choose that. If we see we are making choices that don't make the most out of the moment, we can choose differently. When we choose to experience the present moment rather than the mind's commentary about it, our experience of life changes.

SEE BEAUTY EVERYWHERE

Every moment has the beauty we all long for if we are willing to notice that beauty. Essence sees the beauty in everything, while the ego glides over everything it has seen before as if those things didn't exist. The ego discounts what it sees, while Essence really sees what it sees. When we are aligned with Essence and we really see something, we experience an opening of our Heart and a loving of what we are seeing, no matter what it looks like. And when Essence does something, Essence is really involved in doing it, and doing it is surprisingly pleasurable! The ego has its ideas of pleasure, but those ideas are only occasionally met by life. Meanwhile, the ego misses out on the pleasure and beauty that are available in anything we do, if only we give what we do our full attention.

DO WHAT YOU ARE DOING

Resistance to what we are doing is often caused by a subtle sense that doing something else is more important or more necessary. Subtly, unconsciously, we often diminish in our minds the importance of certain activities, such as picking up around the house, taking the dog out, taking a shower, or going to the grocery store, as if these activities aren't part of life, or shouldn't be. We move through many of our routine activities unconsciously, that is, without being present to them, and often with resentment or a sense that they are causing us to miss out on doing something more worthwhile, meaningful, or fun. What we may not realize is that the lack of bringing our full attention to the activity, or lack of being present to it, is the cause of our discontentment or boredom with it, not the activity itself.

HOW DO YOU CREATE STRESS?

Stress is the sense of contraction that happens when we believe the negative stories our egoic mind is telling us about ourselves, life, other people, the past, or the future. The irony is we think we need these thoughts to function when, in fact, they interfere with handling life and make whatever we're doing less enjoyable. Stress isn't caused by circumstances, although it often coincides with some circumstance or event. It simply comes from the negative interpretation the egoic mind gives life in its ongoing commentary about it.

TUNE IN TO ESSENCE

Essence's channel may not come in as clearly as the ego's channel at first because Essence communicates more subtly and not as loudly as the ego. But as we get better at tuning in to Essence's channel, the signal gets stronger, and the egoic mind's chatter becomes softer. One channel is the Stress Channel and the other is the Peace Channel. We really do have a choice about what we listen to. The Peace Channel can only be heard when we are present in the moment, when we are in the Now. To tune in to the Peace Channel, all we have to do is *be, experience, notice,* and *naturally respond* to what is arising in the moment. To tune into the Stress Channel, we just have to start believing our thoughts again. The great news is we have control over our level of stress. Eliminating stress is just a matter of tuning out the negative and tuning in the positive and just being, experiencing, and dancing to that music instead of the mind's chatter.

PROBLEMS ARE IMAGINARY

The egoic mind imagines a problem, and then it imagines a solution. When we get caught up in these thoughts, we feel like we have a problem that has to be solved before we can be happy. But the problem is just imagined! When we drop out of involvement with these thoughts and into the simple experience of the present moment, we discover that everything is fine just the way it is. Life never had to be any different than it is, nor do we. We can be the "imperfect" human that we are. In fact, we weren't designed to be anything other than the human being that we are. We are doing this human being thing perfectly!

RELAX AND ENJOY THE RIDE

The beauty is that we are all evolving toward being more loving and aligned with the spiritual being that we are, whether we realize that or not. So we can just relax and enjoy the ride that Life is taking us on. All that Life asks is that we choose love over fear and hatred. Fortunately, we all learn that being loving is the only sane choice, since the opposite only leads to suffering. We can't really make a mistake, so nothing needs fixing, because we are all being swept along toward seeing the truth about ourselves and life— that we are all One and life is good!

WHAT STORY ARE YOU RELATING TO?

We bring a story into nearly every moment, and that affects how we experience the moment and how we respond. We have stories about our loved ones, such as: "You don't care about me." "You're not attractive enough for me." "I can't live without you." These stories, the more they are repeated and reinforced, interfere with being present to the people we love, and they are never the whole truth. Rather than responding to our loved ones purely, we let our view of them or our relationship, our story, affect how we react to them. To get the most out of the relationship you are in, it won't be helpful to listen to the ego's stories about it. They will only bring separation and conflict. Essence would tell a different story about your loved one. What might its story be? It would probably be something like: "This person is in my life for me to love to the best of my ability. Let's see what happens if I do that." As Essence, we are here to serve others and serve life. The ego, on the other hand, is all about serving itself.

145

BE AWAKE NOW

The good news is you don't have to have a spiritual awakening to experience awakeness. If you want to experience what it's like to be awakened, then just be here right now and not in your thoughts about the present, the past, the future, or what you want. Just *be* here right now. Do you want awakening enough to give up—ignore—your thoughts about yourself and your desires, which are just more thoughts? That's all that is required, really. Do you want awakening enough to just be present in the moment?

THE BEING YOU ARE IS HERE NOW

The process of awakening is a process of learning to dis-identify with the egoic mind and identify instead with the Being that you are, who is here right now and always has been, looking out of your eyes and breathing and moving your body. Who else would be doing these things? The *you* that you *think* you are stops existing as soon as you stop thinking, so how can that be who you are? The false self, or ego, comes and goes with thoughts about *me, my* life, and what *I* want. When you are involved with thoughts about *me,* you exist as the *me;* when you aren't, you exist as Awakeness, as Essence.

MOVE ON

A lot of things are inherent in life—change, birth, death, aging, illness, accidents, calamities, and losses of all kinds—but these events don't have to be a cause of ongoing suffering. Yes, these events can cause grief and sadness, but grief and sadness pass, like everything else, and are replaced with other experiences. The ego, however, clings to negative thoughts and feelings and, as a result, magnifies, intensifies, and sustains those emotions. Meanwhile, the ego overlooks the subtle feelings of joy, gratitude, excitement, adventure, love, and peace that come from Essence. If we dwelt on these positive feeling states as much as we generally dwell on our negative thoughts and painful emotions, our lives would be transformed.

COMMIT TO NOW

The ego doesn't want to commit to anything—a place, a relationship, a career— because it believes that something better may be possible, and it is willing to forgo what is present for the possibility of something better that isn't present. Essence, on the other hand, is committed to whatever *is*. It doesn't commit into the future because all that exists is the present, so it commits itself to that. That is the essential difference between the ego and Essence: The ego dreams of something better in the midst of whatever is, while Essence simply enjoys and commits attention and love to whatever is. In fact, committing attention to anything that is present results in enjoyment. The ego enjoys so little because it commits attention to what isn't present and to what it doesn't have, and suffers over that, instead of committing attention to whatever is. It loves its fantasies, dreams, and desires more than it loves reality.

NOTICE HOW UNTRUE YOUR THOUGHTS ARE

Once you are aware of your thoughts, you can evaluate them. You can ask, "Is that true?" What is able to be aware of and evaluate our thoughts is Essence. One way Essence liberates us from the tyranny of the egoic mind is through our capacity to notice and evaluate our thoughts. This capacity belongs to Essence. Ignoring our thoughts becomes much easier once we learn to notice them and when we see how untrue, irrelevant, and negative they are. If your thoughts are untrue, irrelevant, and negative, why would you give them your attention? Seeing how false and unhelpful our thoughts are naturally frees us from them.

GIVE UP THOUGHTS THAT MAKE YOU FEEL BAD

Truly, the only thing in the way of experiencing the peace and ease of Essence is believing the ego's lies, the seemingly harmless and seemingly true thoughts that constantly float through our minds, which appear to be our thoughts. But these thoughts aren't ours; they belong to the false self. They aren't Essence's experience of life. When we are able to break through the spell cast by these thoughts and the sense of limited self spun by them, we experience the truth, and the truth is good! When you feel good, you are aligned with your true nature, and when you feel bad you aren't. What a wonderful Homing device we have built into us! Try giving up all the thoughts that make you feel bad, or even just some of them, and see how doing that changes your life. You don't need negative thoughts. All they have ever given you was a false self that suffers. They are all lies.

DON'T SUFFER OVER SUFFERING

People suffer tremendously over the fact that they're suffering, especially when the goal of the spiritual search is to end all suffering, then not suffering becomes just one more goal to fail at for the ego to suffer over. Resisting your suffering can cause just as much suffering as resisting whatever else you are resisting about life, which caused the suffering in the first place. Being upset because you are suffering holds the initial suffering in place and prolongs it. Once you see this, there is the possibility of just allowing the suffering you are experiencing to be here, for now. If it's here, then let it be here. That acceptance will provide an environment where the contraction you are feeling can begin to relax.

SUFFERING ISN'T A PROBLEM

When suffering is no longer seen as a problem, then it can come and go. When it shows up, it is an opportunity to see through any mistaken beliefs and negativity. Weather is part of life, and as long as you are human, so is contraction and expansion of consciousness part of life. Whether you suffer over contraction or not is a matter of how much acceptance you bring to it when it is happening and how much compassion and tenderness you give yourself for being human. The solution to suffering is acceptance, compassion, gentleness, and love for yourself and others who are temporarily believing the ego's negativity.

ORIENT YOURSELF TOWARD YOUR BEING

The Being that you are, which is content with life, doesn't communicate with you through thought, but through a sense of happiness, completeness, peace, joy, relaxation (ahhhh), and pleasure. When you feel that way, you are experiencing life truly, as the Being that you are (Essence) experiences life. The more you orient yourself toward sensations and positive feelings and away from negative thoughts and thoughts about yourself, the more you will experience yourself as that Being instead of the false self. You are not what you think you are, what you like, what you want, what you imagine yourself to be, or what others imagine you to be. You are far grander than those ideas about yourself. Begin to see the greatness of this Being that you are, and you will begin to enjoy this life, even the challenges. Find that which is within you that enjoys life.

TRUST HOME

When we land in this place of Home we recognize it, and we don't want to leave it; and yet, we do. Something always calls us away, and that is the mind: thoughts about something, anything. Instead of bringing us Home, our thoughts take us away from it. Our thoughts seem so important and necessary, and they are so enticing. The ego is what calls us away from Home because it doesn't trust this place of calm, peace, safety, and completion. The ego runs from the incomprehensible, the inexplicable, and what nourishes us, not because it doesn't want to be nourished, but because it doesn't trust that this place actually provides what it does. When you finally drop all striving and come Home, do you trust this place? Do you recognize it? Do you value it? Do you want to know how to spend more time there? Unless we do trust this place, recognize it, value it, and desire to experience it, we won't stay there.

THE PAST AND FUTURE ARE
IMAGINARY

The past is a diluted memory, and the future is a figment of the ego's imagination. The past and future only exist as thoughts. The ego creates a sense of time through thoughts about the past and the future, and we can become entranced by the ego's world when we believe these thoughts *are* the past and future. What we imagine can seem very real, especially when those imaginations create feelings, which make our thoughts seem even more real. The painful feelings related to a loss often come more from what we tell ourselves about the loss than from the loss itself, especially the farther away in time we get from the loss.

ABOUT THE AUTHOR

Gina Lake is a spiritual teacher and the author of numerous books about awakening to one's true nature, including *From Stress to Stillness*, *Trusting Life*, *Embracing the Now*, *Radical Happiness*, *Living in the Now*, *Return to Essence*, *Loving in the Moment*, *Anatomy of Desire*, and *Getting Free*. She is also a gifted intuitive with a master's degree in counseling psychology and over twenty years experience supporting people in their spiritual growth. Her website offers information about her books and courses, free e-books, book excerpts, a monthly newsletter, a blog, and audio and video recordings:

www.radicalhappiness.com

Other Books by Gina Lake

(Available in paperback, Kindle, and other e-book formats.)

Embracing the Now: Finding Peace and Happiness in What Is. The Now—this moment—is the true source of happiness and peace and the key to living a fulfilled and meaningful life. *Embracing the Now* is a collection of essays that can serve as daily reminders of the deepest truths. Full of clear insight and wisdom, *Embracing the Now* explains how the mind keeps us from being in the moment, how to move into the Now and stay there, and what living from the Now is like. It also explains how to overcome stumbling blocks to being in the Now, such as fears, doubts, misunderstandings, judgments, distrust of life, desires, and other conditioned ideas that are behind human suffering.

From Stress to Stillness: Tools for Inner Peace. Most stress is created by how we think about things. *From Stress to Stillness* will help you to examine what you are thinking and change your relationship to your thoughts so that they no longer result in stress. Drawing from the wisdom traditions, psychology, New Thought, and the author's own experience as a spiritual teacher and counselor, *From Stress to Stillness* offers many practices and suggestions that will lead to greater peace and equanimity, even in a busy and stress-filled world.

Radical Happiness: A Guide to Awakening provides the keys to experiencing the happiness that is ever-present and not dependent on circumstances. This happiness doesn't come from getting what you want, but from wanting what is here now. It comes from realizing that who you think you are is not who you really are. This is a radical perspective! *Radical Happiness* describes the nature of the egoic state of consciousness and how it interferes with happiness, what awakening and enlightenment are, and how to live in the world after awakening.

Trusting Life: Overcoming the Fear and Beliefs That Block Peace and Happiness. Fear and distrust keep us from living the life we were meant to live, and they are the greatest hurdles to seeing the truth about life—that it is good, abundant, supportive, and potentially joyous. *Trusting Life* is a deep exploration into the mystery of who we are, why we suffer, why we don't trust life, and how to become more trusting. It offers evidence that life is trustworthy and tools for overcoming the fear and beliefs that keep us from falling in love with life.

Loving in the Moment: Moving from Ego to Essence in Relationships. Having a truly meaningful relationship requires choosing love over your conditioning, that is, your ideas, fantasies, desires, images, and beliefs. *Loving in the Moment* describes how to move beyond conditioning, judgment, anger, romantic illusions, and differences to the experience of love and Oneness with another. It explains how to drop into the core of your Being, where Oneness and love exist, and be with others from there.

Anatomy of Desire: How to Be Happy Even When You Don't Get What You Want will help you discriminate between your Heart's desires and the ego's and to relate to the ego's desires in a way that reduces suffering and increases joy. By pointing out the myths about desire that keep us tied to our ego's desires and the suffering they cause, *Anatomy of Desire* will help you be happy regardless of your desires and whether you are attaining them. So it is also about spiritual freedom, or liberation, which comes from following the Heart, our deepest desires, instead of the ego's desires. It is about becoming a lover of life rather than a desirer.

Return to Essence: How to Be in the Flow and Fulfill Your Life's Purpose describes how to get into the flow and stay there and how to live life from there. Being in the flow and not being in the flow are two very different states. One is dominated by the ego-driven mind, which is the cause of suffering, while the other is the domain of Essence, the Divine within each of us. You are meant to live in the flow. The flow is the experience of Essence—your true self—as it lives life through you and fulfills its purpose for this life.

Living in the Now: How to Live as the Spiritual Being That You Are. The 99 essays in *Living in the Now* will help you realize your true nature and live as that. They answer many question raised by the spiritual search and offer wisdom on subjects such as fear, anger, happiness, aging, boredom, desire, patience, faith, forgiveness, acceptance, love, commitment, hope, purpose, meaning, meditation, being present, emotions, trusting life, trusting your Heart, and many other deep subjects. These essays will help you become more conscious, present, happy, loving, grateful, at peace, and fulfilled. Each essay stands on its own and can be used for daily contemplation.

Getting Free: How to Move Beyond Conditioning and Be Happy. Freedom from your conditioning is possible, but the mind is a formidable opponent to freedom. To be free requires a new way of thinking or, rather, not thinking. To a large extent, healing our conditioning involves changing our relationship to our mind and discovering who we really are. *Getting Free* will help you do that. It will also help you reprogram your mind; clear negative thoughts and self-images; use meditation, prayer, forgiveness, and gratitude; work with spiritual forces to assist healing and clear negativity; and heal entrenched issues from the past.

For more info, please visit the "Books" page at
www.radicalhappiness.com

What About Now?

Made in the USA
San Bernardino, CA
02 September 2013